mat. # 800063

J
B
ONE

12,459

W9-BEM-446

BLOOMFIELD PUBLIC LIBRARY
New Bloomfield, PA   17068

purchase 15.95 MidAmerica Books 2003

BLOOMFIELD PUBLIC LIBRARY
New Bloomfield, PA   17068

12,459

Jam Session

Shaquille O'Neal

Terri Dougherty

ABDO Publishing Company

visit us at
www.abdopub.com

Published by ABDO Publishing Company, 4940 Viking Drive, Suite 622, Edina, Minnesota 55435. Copyright © 2001 by Abdo Consulting Group, Inc. International copyrights reserved in all countries. No part of this book may be reproduced in any form without written permission from the publisher.

Printed in the United States.

Cover and Interior Photo credits: AP Wide World Photos; All-Sport Photos

Edited by Denis Dougherty

Book design: Patrick Laurel

Sources: Associated Press; Newsweek; New York Daily News; People Magazine; Sports Illustrated; Sports Illustrated For Kids; Time Magazine; ESPN Magazine; USA Today

Library of Congress Cataloging-in-Publication Data

Dougherty, Terri.
    Shaquille O'Neal / Terri Dougherty.
        p.   cm. -- (Jam Session)
    Includes index.
      ISBN 1-57765-471-4
    1. O'Neal, Shaquille--Juvenile literature. 2. Basketball players--United States--Biography--Juvenile literature. [1. O'Neal, Shaquille. 2. Basketball players. 3. Afro-Americans--Biography.]   I. Title. II. Series.

    GV884.054 D68 2001
    796.323'092--dc21
    [B]

                                                                        00-045378

Contents

The Ultimate Shaq Attack

*S*haquille O'Neal is known for heaving his 7-foot-1, 315-pound body into the air for crushing dunks. Off the court, he soars as a rapper, actor, and product pitchman. But until the 2000 NBA Finals, the big man lacked one big thing: a championship.

Shaq's Los Angeles Lakers and the Indiana Pacers were facing off in Game 6 of the NBA Finals at the Staples Center in Los Angeles. The Lakers had hoped to clinch the series in the previous game, but instead had been embarrassed by a 33-point loss in Indianapolis.

"I think we played a little too loose, a little too happy, and they just hit shots," Shaq said. "When they're shooting like that, especially at home, we knew it was going to be hard."

Shaq was all too familiar with losing in the postseason. He had never won an NBA championship, and the Lakers had been swept out of the playoffs the previous two seasons. He had also been on the wrong end of series sweeps three times with his former team, the Orlando Magic, including the 1995 NBA Finals.

But this was Shaq's year. He had dominated the league all season and finished as the league leader in points per game, with a 29.7 average. He was also first in field goal percentage at .574, second in rebounds with a 13.6 average, and third in blocks, averaging 3.03 a game. He was the MVP of the regular season and co-MVP of the All-Star Game.

In Game 6 of the Finals, sharpshooting guard Reggie Miller and the Pacers led for much of the game. Just when the Lakers would get close, Indiana would surge ahead. But this time, Shaq simply refused to lose. He dominated the basket area as he had all season. He overpowered the overmatched Indiana big men for hoop after hoop at one end. He intimidated any Pacers player who dared to drive to the basket. He swatted away shots and gobbled up rebounds.

Shaq overpowers the Indiana defense during Game 4 of the 2000 NBA Finals.

With the broadest shoulders in basketball carrying them, the Lakers finally took control. The game was tied at 103 with five minutes left, but Shaq made a 10-footer from the baseline and a free throw to help the Lakers take the lead, 110-107, with 1:56 left. Free throws by fellow superstar Kobe Bryant in the game's final seconds clinched the 116-111 victory. The Lakers had their first championship since 1988, and Shaq had his first since high school.

After the game, Shaq hugged Bryant and cried, washing away the years of struggle. "I've held the emotion for about 11 years— three years in college and eight years in the league," Shaq said. "It just came out."

Shaq had 41 points in the game. He averaged 38 points and 16.7 rebounds in the series and was named the Finals MVP. "This is what I wanted to come to the NBA for," Shaq said. "I worked very hard to get here, and it was an emotional game. I'm very happy."

Opposite page: Shaq enjoying a rare moment on the bench.

Little Big Man

When Shaq was born, Lucille O'Neal took a look at her 7-pound, 13-ounce baby and gave him the name Shaquille Rashaun, which means "Little Warrior" in Islam. "That's what I wanted him to be, a warrior," she said. "I wanted him to be strong, independent, and tough."

The early years were tough for Shaq and his mom. Shaq's dad left when Shaq was a few months old. His mom worked for the city of Newark, New Jersey, and they lived with his mom's grandmother.

Then Lucille met Philip Harrison, who also worked for the city of Newark, and they married when Shaq was two years old. Harrison joined the army to better provide for his family, which grew to include Lateefah, Ayesha, and Jamal.

Shaq always thought of "The Sarge" as his dad, and learned about hard work from the Army staff sergeant, who held down as many as three jobs at a time to support his family. "I didn't have a lot," Shaq said, "but I had what I needed."

Shaq wasn't a perfect child. As a youth he often tested his parents' patience. "Shaquille was a typical boy—rough, outgoing, busy," Lucille said. "If you said, 'Shaquille, don't light that match because the match might cause a fire,' when you turned your head, he would light it to see if it caused a fire."

Philip's firm discipline helped Shaq get through this difficult phase. "Nobody really knew if I was going to come through it or not," Shaq said. "I used to do bad stuff. Not bad stuff like killing or drugs or anything like that. But anything below that, I did it."

Still, his mom knew she could depend on him. One night, when Philip was away on a military assignment, Shaq, his mother, and two younger sisters were driving from Newark to Jersey City. They got a flat tire, and Shaq's mom was scared. She got out of the car, sat next to the curb, and cried.

"Shaquille came over to me, after trying to fix the tire himself, and said, 'Mommy, it's going to be OK,'" she said. "Then, by the grace of God, a man came by and changed the tire for me. Shaquille was my rock back then when my husband wasn't home. He stuck by me."

Philip was Shaq's first coach. Shaq tried football first, and won all three phases of a Punt, Pass, and Kick competition at age nine.

"I thought I was something," Shaq said. "Then Dad told me, 'Don't get the big head.'" Shaq played football until a little muscular opponent tackled him in the knee. Then he decided to concentrate on basketball.

"Dr. J was my hero. I tried to do the stuff he used to do," Shaq said of the acrobatic Julius Erving of the Philadelphia 76ers. "Dad told me, 'Son, being Dr. J is good, but you can't be Dr. J. There's only one Dr. J. You want to be yourself.'"

Philip's military career took the family to many different places. The family moved from New Jersey to Georgia to West Germany to San Antonio, Texas. While the family was living in West Germany, Shaq was cut from his ninth grade basketball team. His father told him not to give up. "When I needed to talk about important things, he was there," Shaq said. "Phil is the one I looked up to."

When Shaq was 13, Louisiana State University basketball coach Dale Brown visited the military base in Wildflecken, West Germany, where Harrison was stationed. He saw Shaq, who was then 13 and 6-foot-8, and asked what his rank was. "No rank," Shaq replied. "I'm 13 years old."

Brown quickly tracked down Shaq's dad. They struck up a friendship that resulted in Shaq going to college at LSU. But before college, Shaq had to finish high school. The family moved to San Antonio, where Shaq led Cole High to a 68-1 record in two seasons. In his senior year, the team went 38-0 and won the Class AAA state title. Then it was time to move on to LSU, and introduce the nation to the Shaq Attack.

Opposite page: Shaq being interviewed after his team won the Texas high school championship.

This Tiger is Grrrrrrreat!

*S*haq was a tough player as a freshman. Some NBA scouts said he would have been a top draft choice if he had left the school in the spring after his freshman year. "There's no comparison to him as a freshman," said Eddie Fogler, Vanderbilt's coach at the time.

Shaq attracted attention even though his play was often overshadowed during his freshman season by guard Chris Jackson, one of the nation's leading scorers, and fellow big man Stanley Roberts. Both left the Tigers after Shaq's freshman year, giving him more room to display his talents.

Shaq liked to provide extra excitement in games by trying to rip the basketball goal apart with one of his jams. In a mid-November exhibition game, against the Newscastle (Australia) Falcons, he did a two-handed dunk in LSU's Maravich Assembly Center that moved the basket base and broke the chain anchoring it to the floor.

He was only 18, but was called the nation's best big man. Against No. 2-ranked Arizona, he scored 16 points in the final six minutes of the game, including a final rim-hanging dunk, to lead the Tigers to a 92-82 win. Shaq dominated the game finishing with 29 points, 14 rebounds, and six blocks.

During the season, Shaq worked out with two of the greatest centers ever, Bill Walton and Kareem Abdul-Jabbar, to polish his game. He finished the season with 140 blocked shots, and averaged 27.6 points and 14.7 rebounds while shooting .628 from the field.

"This guy may have the physical talent and personal discipline to be the best ever," Walton said.

"He just overpowers people," said Joe Dean, LSU's athletic director and a former star player. "I've never seen men 7 feet tall, 300 pounds who could run the floor like he does. He took a ball off the defensive board against Kentucky last year, went coast to coast and laid it in. You don't see that kind of maneuverability with this kind of size."

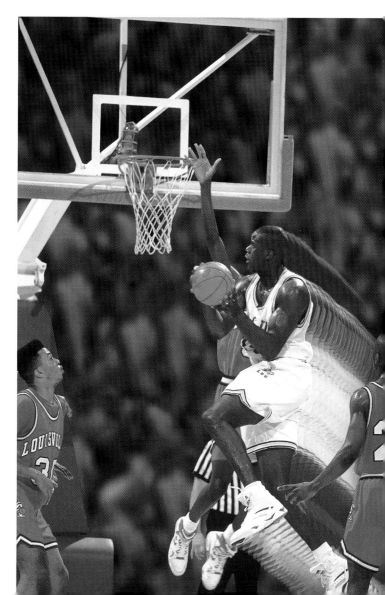

Shaq going in for a lay-up while playing for LSU.

Magic Man

Shaq decided to enter the NBA Draft in 1992 instead of staying at LSU for his senior season. It was no surprise that he was the top pick, chosen by the Orlando Magic. Right away, Shaq showed he was going to make an impact in the NBA. In his first game, he grabbed 18 rebounds. He became the first player to be named NBA Player of the Week in his first week in the league.

Shaq played in the All-Star Game, and was Rookie of the Year. The Magic went 41-41, after going 21-61 the previous season. The Magic's superstar was just as much of a sensation off the court. He appeared in the movie "Blue Chips" with Nick Nolte, earning $1 million for his off-season job. He cut a rap song and made a number of advertisements, earning $30 million for endorsements.

Although Shaq was criticized for the way he barreled through the lane and his lack of a shooting touch, there was no denying he was a force to be reckoned with. During his first two years in the league, he dunked 709 times in 162 games. In 1993-94, he led the Magic to its first playoff appearance.

"Obviously, he's a great, great, great young talent," said Jerry West, the Lakers executive vice president for basketball operations. "You watch him and you see things in his future that kind of open your eyes. He has all the things necessary to really be an impact player for years to come. You wonder where he'll be when he matures and plays at the level everybody expects him to get to."

Taking on the World

After the 1993-94 season, Shaq returned to LSU to take classes toward a business degree and work on his offensive moves. During the summer of 1994, he won a gold medal with USA Basketball at the World Championships in Toronto. He led the team in scoring and rebounding, and coaches said he was one of the hardest-working players in practice. He carried that confidence into the next season.

"He's playing with a more dominant attitude," Magic general manager Pat Williams said. "More confidence. A sharper focus."

That season the Magic added Horace Grant, a power forward from the Chicago Bulls. Shaq, Horace, and the previous year's addition of Anfernee (Penny) Hardaway, gave the Magic one of the best teams in the NBA.

"We've got the pieces we wanted, and now we want to win a championship," Shaq said.

Shaq continued to try to solve his biggest problem, free-throw shooting. He reached a career low and consulted with a shot doctor, golfer, astrologer, eye doctor, and relaxation expert.

"I'm trying my hardest, but I can't have everything," he said. "I can't have the looks, rapping ability, scoring ability, and shoot free throws. But I'm going to hit them one day."

Despite his one downfall, it looked like Shaq and the Magic had enough talent to make it to the top. In the Eastern Conference semifinals, the Magic defeated Chicago 4-2, even though the great Michael Jordan had returned to the Bulls toward the end of that season. Orlando beat Indiana 4-3 in the conference finals, and met defending champion Houston Rockets in the NBA Finals.

Shaq played well, averaging 28 points and 12.5 rebounds a game, but Orlando was swept. Shaq would have to wait for his title.

Orlando Magic superstars, Anfernee Hardaway (left) and Shaquille O'Neal take a breather during the NBA Finals. Both players have since left the Magic for different teams. Hardaway is now a Phoenix Sun and Shaq has become a Laker.

Hello, Hollywood

Expectations were high the next season, and the Magic had a great year going 60-22. The Magic beat the Detroit Pistons and the Atlanta Hawks in the first two rounds of the playoffs. But in the conference finals the Magic faced a Chicago team that had the best record in league history at 72-10. Shaq did his part, averaging 27 points and 10.8 rebounds against Chicago, but the Bulls swept the Magic in four games.

After the season, it was time for a change. Shaq signed with the Los Angeles Lakers, bringing the multitalented big man to the town that could appreciate all of his assets. Shaq was no stranger to L.A. He had been there to work out with other players and make movies. Unlike in Orlando, his every move wouldn't be closely watched. Around Los Angeles and Hollywood, he was a star in a universe of celebrities.

Shaq kept busy doing commercials, recording rap albums, and making appearances, but not on game days. He only made movies during the summer, and even then he practiced free throws and played basketball for hours. "He works as hard as anybody," said Del Harris, the Lakers coach at the time.

Shaq embraced the community, hosting "Shaqsgiving" and "Shaq-a Clause" celebrations. "He's one of the nicest kids I've ever been around," West said.

By the end of January, the Lakers were in first place in the Pacific Division. Shaq was the only player in the NBA in the top five in scoring, rebounding, shooting percentage, and blocks. He averaged 26.2 points per game for the season. In the playoffs, Shaq led the Lakers with 26.9 points, 10.6 rebounds, and 1.89 blocked shots per game, but Los Angeles was eliminated by Utah in the 1997 Western Conference semifinals.

The next season, the Lakers advanced a step further, to the conference finals. But the Utah Jazz swept Los Angeles in four games. The 1999 playoffs also ended in disappointment. The Lakers fell to eventual NBA champion San Antonio Spurs in the conference semifinals. Shaq was happy with his life, but still needed a championship to make his career complete. In the 1999-2000 season, a coaching change made all the difference.

Shaq at his press conference announcing he had signed a contract with the Los Angeles Lakers.

NBA Champs

*P*hil Jackson took over as the Lakers coach before the 1999-2000 season and brought with him his six championship rings he won as coach of the Bulls. Shaq respected Jackson because of what the coach had done in Chicago. Kobe Bryant was becoming a star in his own right, but under Jackson's coaching everyone on the team put egos aside and worked together toward the goal of a championship.

On his 28th birthday, Shaq's teammates gave him a present by helping him score a career-high 61 points in a 123-103 win over the Los Angeles Clippers. After the season, he won the MVP award and was named to the all-NBA first team.

"Shaq has played at such a high level the entire year, and Kobe came in here

The Lakers' dynamic duo, Kobe Bryant (left) and Shaq.

and there was a mutual adjustment," Jackson said. "I like their demeanor. They are starting to play with a lot of poise."

Los Angeles zoomed to an NBA-best 67-15 record. But in the first round of the playoffs, the Sacramento Kings had a chance to upset the Lakers. The series was tied 2-2, but Shaq took charge with 32 points and 18 rebounds in the decisive fifth game. Los Angeles crushed the Kings 113-86.

The Lakers eliminated the Phoenix Suns, 4-1, in the next round to advance to the conference finals against the Portland Trail Blazers. In the deciding Game 7, the Lakers trailed by 13 points after three quarters. But the big man came up big when he was needed most.

Shaq scored nine points in the fourth quarter to lead the Lakers' furious rally. Shaq's thunderous dunk off of a lob pass from Bryant put Los Angeles ahead 85-79 with 40 seconds left, and the Lakers escaped with an 89-84 victory. Shaq, who had made eight of 12 free throws in the game, was back in the NBA Finals.

After his late-game heroics against Portland, the Shaq Diesel just kept on rolling. In the Finals, Indiana had no answer for Shaq's unmatched combination of size, strength, and athletic ability. The Pacers' Rik Smits is nicknamed the "Dunking Dutchman," but Shaq simply turned the 7-4 center into the "Dunked-on Dutchman."

Shaq also showed off the soft touch he had developed in becoming a complete player. He mixed in turnaround jumpers from 10 feet out in addition to his power moves around the basket. "This year, Shaq's been attacking and he's just been great for us all year long," Bryant said.

As the Lakers celebrated their title, Shaq towered over reporters amid the chaos and excitement in the locker room. "There can no longer be any 'buts' surrounding my name," Shaq said. "Now that we have one (title), we just have to work on two, three, four, five. It's everything I thought it would be."

Shaq and Kobe celebrate after winning the NBA Championship.

Shaquille O'Neal Profile

Born: March 6, 1972

Height: 7-foot-1

Weight: 315 pounds

Position: Center

Number: 34

College: Louisiana State University

Residence: Beverly Hills, California

Family: Daughter, Taahirah;
  parents, Lucille and Philip
  Harrison; two sisters, Lateefah
  and Ayesha; one brother, Jamal.

Personal: His first and middle names, Shaquille Rashaun, mean "Little Warrior" in Islam ... Has released five rap albums ... Has been in movies, starring in "Kazaam," appearing in "Blue Chips," and making a cameo in "He Got Game"... Owns a record label and clothing line entitled "TWIsM"... As Shaq-a-Claus, purchased toys to distribute at Christmas to disadvantaged youths ... Served as Shaq-a-Bunny for Easter.

Honors

1999-00 - NBA Most Valuable Player, falling one vote short of becoming the first unanimous winner in NBA history.

2000 - NBA All-Star Game co-MVP, sharing the honor with San Antonio's Tim Duncan after getting 22 points and nine rebounds.

2000 - Finals MVP, a unanimous choice, becoming the third NBA player to win All-Star Game, regular season, and Finals MVP in the same season (The New York Knicks' Willis Reed in 1970 and the Chicago Bulls' Michael Jordan in 1996 and 1998 are the others).

1999-00 - All-NBA first-team pick, a unanimous selection.

1999-00 - Leads NBA in scoring (29.7) and field-goal percentage (.574).

1999-00 - Second-team choice on all-NBA defensive team.

1998-99 - All-NBA second-team pick.

1998-99 - Leads NBA in field-goal percentage (.576).

1997-98 - All-NBA first-team selection.

1997-98 - Leads NBA in field-goal percentage (.584).

1996-97 - All-NBA third-team choice despite missing 31 games due to injury.

1996 - Selected as one of the 50 Greatest Players in NBA history.

1996 - Member of the Dream Team that won the gold medal at the Olympics in Atlanta.

1995-96 - All-NBA third-team pick despite missing first third of season with broken thumb.

BLOOMFIELD PUBLIC LIBRARY
New Bloomfield, PA   17068

1994-95 - All-NBA second-team selection.

1994-95 - Leads NBA in scoring (29.3 points per game).

1994 - Member of the United States team that won the World Championship of Basketball in Toronto.

1993-94 - All-NBA third-team pick.

1993-94 - Leads NBA in field-goal percentage (.599).

1992-93 - NBA Rookie of the Year.

1992-93 - Named to all-rookie first team.

1992 - Became first player in NBA history to be named Player of the Week in his first week in league in November.

1991-92 - Leads nation in blocked shots per game (5.2).

1991-92 - First team all-America pick.

1990-91 - Named national Player of the Year in most polls as a sophomore at LSU.

1990-91 - First team all-America pick.

Shaq holding the NBA Finals and Finals MVP trophies.

12,459

Chronology

March 6, 1972 - Shaquille O'Neal is born in Newark, New Jersey.

1988-89 - Leads Cole High School of San Antonio to undefeated season and Texas Class AAA state title.

1990-91 - As a sophomore at LSU, he averages 27.6 points and 14.7 rebounds while shooting .628 from the floor. His rebounding average leads the nation, and he's named national Player of the Year in most polls.

1992 - Taken by the Orlando Magic with the first pick in the NBA Draft.

1992-93 - Leads Magic to 41-41 record, a 20-game improvement over the previous season.

November 20, 1993 - Grabs 28 rebounds and blocks 15 shots, still career-high totals, against the New Jersey Nets.

1993-94 - Leads Orlando to its first playoff appearance, but Magic is swept by Indiana.

1994-95 - Leads Orlando to 57-25 record, the best in the Eastern Conference, and into the NBA Finals. The Magic is swept by Houston in the Finals.

1995-96 - Leads Orlando to Eastern Conference finals, but Magic is swept by Chicago.

1996 - Signs seven-year, $120 million contract as a free agent with the Los Angeles Lakers.

2000 - Scores career-high 61 points vs. Los Angeles Clippers on March 6, his 28th birthday.

June, 2000 - Leads Lakers to their first NBA title since 1988.

Shaquille O'Neal's stats

Season	Team	MPG	FG%	FT%	RPG.	APG.	SPG.	BPG.	PPG
1992-93	Orlando	37.9	.562	.592	13.9	1.9	.74	3.53	23.4
1993-94	Orlando	39.8	.599	.554	13.2	2.4	.94	2.85	29.3
1994-95	Orlando	37.0	.583	.533	11.4	2.7	.92	2.43	29.3
1995-96	Orlando	36.0	.573	.487	11.0	2.9	.63	2.13	26.6
1996-97	L.A.	38.1	.557	.484	12.5	3.1	.90	2.88	26.2
1997-98	L.A.	36.3	.584	.527	11.4	2.4	.65	2.40	28.3
1998-99	L.A.	34.8	.576	.540	10.7	2.3	.73	1.67	26.3
1999-00	L.A.	40.0	.574	.524	13.6	3.8	.46	3.03	29.7
Career	Orl./L.A.	37.7	.577	.534	12.4	2.7	.75	2.69	27.5
Playoffs (89 games)		39.7	.569	.500	12.2	3.2	.69	2.17	27.7
All-Star games (six)		24.7	.494	.477	7.8	1.0	.83	1.83	17.2

KEY:

MPG - Minutes per game

FG% - Field-goal percentage

FT% - Free-throw percentage

RPG - Rebounds per game

APG - Assists per game

SPG - Steals per game

BPG - Blocked shots per game

PPG - Points per game

Glossary

CONFERENCE - A group of athletic teams that compete against each other for a championship.

DEFICIT - The amount by which something falls short.

DRAFT - The process by which professional sports teams choose new players.

DUNK - To slam a ball through the basket.

FREE THROW - A shot from behind the foul line a player takes without being guarded. A player is awarded free throws after being fouled by another player.

MVP - Most Valuable Player. An award given to the top player in the NBA each season.

NATIONAL BASKETBALL ASSOCIATION (NBA) - A group of teams competing at the highest level of professional basketball.

PLAYOFFS - Games played after the regular season to determine the league champion.

REBOUND - To grab the ball after a missed shot.

SHOOTING PERCENTAGE - How well a player shoots from the floor (not counting free throws). The percentage is determined by dividing the number of shots made by the number of shots taken.

SWEEP - To win or lose all the games in a series.

Index